Story
Ideas

For Mystery Writers

Written
By
Nigel D. Salmon

Story
Ideas

For Mystery writers

Author's website:
www.NigeldSalmon.com

Nigel D. Salmon

Contents

Preface

Everyone who writes a story must begin from an idea. Whether it is fiction or nonfiction, there first has to be the idea for the account and then the idea of how to portray it.

An idea is a conspicuously powerful tool. Everything created has originated from it.

In definition, an idea is a thought for action or speech. Thought is thinking. Thinking is the function of brain-consciousness that controls action and speech.

The term 'story idea' is simplified as the idea for a story.

This book contains ten story ideas under the fascinating genre of Mystery. The genre of Mystery is in the top five in motion pictures and literature. Many famous writers around the world are Mystery writers. If you are desirous of becoming a Mystery writer or probably you just want to try your hand at writing Mystery, you have chosen the right book to read. With each story idea already bearing the plot and conclusion, it should be easy for you to turn any of them into a full story with just the inclusion of dialogues, settings, and even more characters.

And if you always struggle to turn a story idea into a full story, see my book **How To Write Fiction and Nonfiction**, which is a complete guide for new and published authors.

Recommended for those who portray stories through motion pictures and books, this literary work provides story ideas for those who are struggling to come up with good ones. Ten story ideas do not sound even to me as enough, but the amount will suffice based on the realty that ideas are infinite.

The story ideas by themselves are interesting and will leave the reader with somewhat of the same satisfaction as a full story. The pellucid difference between the story ideas and full stories is that each story idea is, needless to say, shorter in length.

Defining Mystery

Mystery is a story that deals with a puzzling crime. A crime is committed (usually a murder) and the mystery is created around the questions of when, where, how, who, and why. The reader is given a hero whose duty it is to find the hidden answers to these burning questions. The plot is spiked with innocent but suspicious characters, near catches and escapes, and false trails to zigzag and hamper the solving of the crime to maintain the essential element of 'uncertainty' toward the conclusion.

In this book, as previously stated, you are given ten story ideas for mystery. With each story idea, you are shown the mystery, the plot, and then the conclusion. Can you turn one into a full story?

One

The Dead Wife

The Mystery:

A business woman (Candy) is shot dead in the dining room of her house while eating with her husband. Who killed her? And why?

The Plot:

Candy is married to Robert for the last four years. One evening she finds out that Robert is cheating on her when she reads an email in his Gmail account which he had forgotten to log out of.

That same evening Candy confronts Robert about his infidelity. Robert does not deny it, revealing that he has 'slipped' a couple of times. Candy asks Robert about the large sums of money that has left their joint account without explained reason. Robert admits that he has been giving money to the person he is having the affair with.

Robert is refusing to identify the person he is having the affair with. So Candy decides to take matters into her own hands. The name of the person in the email Robert has been communicating with is Shelly. Candy ponders on the name. There is only one woman in town who she knows by the name Shelly—one of her very own employees.

Candy confronts Shelly at her business place with the accusation. Shelly denies having an affair with Robert. After a heated argument, Candy fires Shelly from her fashion design business. As Shelly walks from the office, she threatens, in the presence of other employees, to get back at Candy for firing her.

A week later Candy decides enough is enough. She cannot get over Robert's infidelity, and she cannot bear to sleep in the same bedroom with him again. So she comes up with a clever plan.

Candy approaches a Mexican named Maris with the plan to kill Robert. Maris is a 34 years old janitor at Candy's fashion design business. He is in the United States illegally from Mexico. Candy promises to give him US$20,000 to kill Robert, plus her promise to keep him as an employee and never reveal his illegal status to immigration. Finding himself in a plight, Maris agrees to kill Robert. Candy gives him a pistol.

The murder plot is simple: While Candy and Robert are eating in the dining room of their large house, Maris is to shoot Robert in the head two times.

On the night when the murder is to happen, Robert and Candy are eating in the dining room. Both can be seen from the street through the transparent window. Now a gun is fired. Someone slumps on the dining table. It is Candy. She is shot; one bullet to the side of the head kills her instantly.

A neighbor watering her front lawn with a hose sees Shelly speeding off in her car from in front the house. Shelly becomes the only suspect and is arrested for the murder of Candy.

Conclusion:

Maris is the killer. He is the one Robert is having an affair with. Maris has decided to kill Candy so he and Robert can freely be together. He has been calling himself Shelly in his emails to Robert in case someone accidently read the emails.

Shelly was in front the house that night of the murder, only because she wanted to convince Robert to let Candy hire her back. She sped off after hearing the gun shot.

Maris is later caught when surveillance footage from the camera from a nearing house shows him throwing the murder weapon into a bin.

Two

The missing chapter

The Mystery:

An author (Lindy Spridon) is found dead inside her home office, killed by a single blow from a metal candle holder. Who wanted her dead?

The Plot:

Lindy is the sole beneficiary of the estates of her recently deceased mother. Since the reading of her mother's will, Lindy has had several bitter arguments with her only sibling, a brother (Michael) that her late mother had considered wasteful and irresponsible.

Just three days before her brutal death, Lindy and Michael had a physical fight. He was arrested and spent one night in jail before been released on bail.

Few hours before she was killed, Lindy's father visited her house to speak about Michael's concerns. But the conversation turned ugly when Lindy accused her father of never taking side with her on anything. She also brought up childhood abuses which she has suffered at his hands and says that she has revealed all the abuses in chapter 10 of her book—reflecting the age she was when he sexually abused her.

Not wishing to argue any further, the father left Lindy's house around 9pm. As he was leaving the house, he saw Michael standing outside the gate. He walked past Michael.

The next morning the father went back to Lindy's house. A call comes into the police station where Detective Martin is. The father claims he has found his daughter dead in her home office. Michael becomes the suspect due to his fights with Lindy. Sights of him outside Lindy's house on the night of the killing lead to his arrest for reasonable suspicion of murder.

Conclusion:

Lindy was killed by her father whose finger prints are found on Lindy's manuscript which is missing the 10th chapter. Lindy was recording a voice note on a small voice recorder when her father re-entered her home to kill her. Unluckily for the father, he never knew of the voice recorder which was recording him telling his daughter he had to kill her and the scream of Lindy before she was struck dead.

Three

Missing From Home

The Mystery

17 years old Marley goes missing after she arrives back at her parents' home one early Wednesday night. Her car was still parked in the garage, the engine running, her blood stained the steering wheel, and there was no trace of her. Where is Marley? Was she killed?

The Plot

Bette and Douglas are Marley's parents. Both parents, in their forties, cannot get along. Bette is squandering and supercilious, and her husband keeps scolding her for her negative behaviour.

Marley goes missing.

Douglas is arrested after police investigators hear a 911 recording of a desperate-sounding Marley saying her father is about to kill her, just minutes before she went missing.

Douglas, a reputable business man, is livid by the arrest. As the days go by, his reputation is tarnished by the widespread belief that he had killed his own daughter. In the meantime, Bette goes on television lying about abuses she and her daughter suffered in silence by Douglas. In his first court appearance, the presiding judge refuses to grant Douglas bail.

Two weeks after the night she went missing Marley's body is found in a river some 3 miles from her parents' home. She has been stabbed to death. Douglas (central character) is doing everything from behind bars with the help of his lawyer to prove his innocence. Then he gets a good piece of news: The condition of Marley's body shows that she was murdered within the last three days. This means that Douglas, who is in jail for the last two weeks, is not her killer.

The charge of murder is dropped and Douglas is set free. Police investigators are struggling to find a new suspect.

Conclusion

Released from jail, Douglas takes on an intense, personal investigation into finding out who killed his daughter. He thoroughly searched his daughter's room and found her diary in which the 17 years old girl wrote everything about her mother's plot.

Instead of going straight to the police, Douglas confronts Bette in the living room of their home with the diary. Having no way of explaining her way out of the claims in the diary, Bette confessed to convincing Marley to call 911, fake her murder and to make it appear she was killed by her father.

Bette goes on to confess that while Douglas was in jail, she killed Marley to get her life insurance and dumped her body in the river. Now Bette pulls a pistol and points it at Douglas with intent to kill him and take the incriminating diary.

The detective on the case and few police officers burst into the living room and commands Bette to drop the pistol. She is now arrested and her confession is all caught on a small recorder hidden in Douglas' shirt pocket.

Four

The Good Priest

<u>The Mystery:</u>

82 years old widower Martha Collins is found dead inside a bathtub at her mansion on a Friday morning. Police concludes that she was drowned. The caregiver, 42 years old Ruth, is arrested for the murder. But did she really kill her elderly employer?

<u>The Plot:</u>

Five years before her own death, Mrs. Collins' husband died at the ripe old age of 96. Bereaved and felt lonely, she began finding comfort from the words of the only priest in town who made regular visits to her home. The priest, 40 years old Thomas Panton, is considered in the town as the ideal comforter in times of sadness and confusion. He is known to be of a pious and humble personality. He knows the Bible well and has the ability to find the right words of advice.

Loved, respected and trusted by the people of the small town, Thomas Panton was the right man Mrs. Collins could think of to encourage her.

Mrs. Collins and her husband were feeble and doddery due to old age and had to hire a caregiver, Ruth, who has been working for the elderly couple for the last 15 years up to Mr. Collins' death and then Mrs. Collins' murder. But Ruth has a troubled past. She had spent three years before in prison for armed robbery and just two years in her job with the elderly Collins, she stole a necklace. She was fired. But forgiving, Mrs. Collins hired her back with the understanding that the cost for the necklace would be deducted from her salary.

Thomas Panton, the priest, was fully aware of Ruth's troubled past. He was the one Ruth had gotten anger management advice from to meliorate her life. During their several sessions of counseling, Ruth told Thomas Panton that she still has the jewelry she had stolen in the armed robbery and that she is hiding it in the Collins' mansion. The jewelry values over three hundred thousand dollars.

Just a week before her murder, Mrs. Collins told Thomas Panton that she is seriously considering changing her will to bequeath the mansion and the land it is on to Ruth. Over the years she has grown to love Ruth and believed that if given some wealth, Ruth would not return to the crime of stealing.

When 50 years old David, the Collins' only son, knew of his mother's intention to change her will, he disagreed but had no legal ground by which to stop her. Though David liked Ruth, he wanted the will to stay the way it was originally written. In its original form, the will gives joint ownership of the estate to David and the priest, Thomas Panton. If changed, the current beneficiaries would be omitted.

Mr. Lawson, the lawyer, was in town the Thursday to discuss the change of the will the next day with Mrs. Collins. David was also in town with his wife, an avaricious and supercilious lady, who was urging him annoyingly to stop his mother from altering the will. Ruth was excited. But Thomas Panton was getting worried, understanding clearly well that his name was to be struck from the will.

The Thursday night David and his wife last conversed with Mrs. Collins at 9:05pm before going back to the left side of the mansion where they were staying for the duration of their visit. Thomas Panton was at the house and left around 9:30pm, leaving Ruth and Mrs. Collins in the master bedroom.

At 5:02 Friday morning an alarm was raised by David who, after making a call to the police, claimed he found his mother lying dead in her bathtub filled and overflowing with water. As the police arrived, David was already angrily accusing Ruth of negligence, soon changing his accusation to that of murder.

Ruth, a portly Black woman, appeared confused. She claimed she last attended Mrs. Collins around 4:50 am and went back to her room to sleep.

As the bathroom became a crime scene, Thomas Panton turned up at the mansion. He mollified David and began emitting words of comfort in this time of tragic lost.

But the death of the elderly woman was apparently a murder, and this meant   that someone in the mansion is the culprit. Difference in facial expressions and emotions is intelligible among the four possible killers as one police investigator, 54 years old Derrick Hampster, began his questioning of everyone in the large living room on the first floor of the ample house. Hampster was convinced that the killer was in his presence, but which of the four? He first needed to establish a motive.

David, though placated from his anger, sat on the long couch beside his wife and looked stricken with grieve and his face pointing mostly to the carpeted floor. His wife appeared rather unperturbed in the distressing situation. She was most delighted on the inside that, with her old and stubborn mother-in-law now dead, the will cannot be changed. Ruth looked despondent while sitting on the long couch still clothed in her white nightdress and a dotty bandanna wrapping the top of her head. Thomas Panton sat at one end of the couch dressed in his priestly apparel and looking and acting within the religious context of his position.

Ruth stood out as the most likely culprit to Hampster. With David's alibi that he was with his wife on the left side of the mansion and Thomas Panton's statement that he had left the mansion around half past 9pm and returned to the Catholic Church, Hampster had to zero in on the caregiver whose criminal record, and history of violent acts, painted her as the most capable doer of the crime. She was taken into custody for the murder.

Conclusion:

Seven hours later while going through all the things collected from the crime scene, Hampster got to understand that Ruth is innocent. The culprit is Thomas Panton.

Panton had managed to coax the elder Mrs. Collins into adding him to her will after the death of her husband. When Mrs. Collins expressed her intention to change the will, Panton knew his plan might be ruined. So he decided to do something about it. Panton usually let himself out of the mansion after each visit. But on the Thursday night, he pretended he had left and hid himself inside the house. He patiently waited till David and his wife went to bed on the left side of the mansion. Knowing that Ruth normally attend to Mrs. Collins two times during the night, he patiently waited till after the last visit the caregiver made to her employer's bedroom before sunrise.

Hampster figured out how the crime was committed as follows:

Thomas Panton entered the victim's bedroom while everyone else was asleep. He took the victim to the bathroom adjacent to her bedroom and drowned her. This was not difficult as Mrs. Collins was a small and feeble old lady. While holding down the victim beneath the surface of the water, Panton never noticed that her fingers pulled off his clerical collar in a desperate but useless attempt to save her own life.

Just seconds after the victim gave up the ghost, Panton heard David coming along the passage outside the bedroom with loud whistling lips. He hurried from the bathroom, hid in the bedroom and as David entered the bathroom he dashed out of the victim's bedroom and the house.

The clerical collar found in the bathtub proved that Thomas Collins committed the crime. A nun at the church said she saw the priest hurrying into the church wet and without his collar. A search of Thomas Panton's bedchamber at the church revealed the jewelry he knew Ruth was hiding at the Collins' mansion. He also stole the jewelry on the night of the murder.

Thomas Panton is arrested and charged for the murder.

Five

The Missing Wife

The Mystery:

34 years old real estate agent Debra Madison went missing after she left home one Monday morning to meet a client. On the evening of the next day her blouse was found beside a lake in the same town of Lashville where she lived. She was assumed dead.

On Thursday, the same week, the body of 40 years old Candy Stewart was discovered on the bank of a road in the same town. She was strangled.

On Sunday morning of the next week Candy's 19 years old daughter was found strangled in the house she shared with her recently deceased mother.

The town of Lashville now has two confirmed murders and an unconfirmed one bearing remarkable similarities. Who was committing these crimes?

The Plot:

Debra Madison and her husband, Joshua, have been married for the past six years and have a 4 years old daughter named Alice. The marriage was harmonious until a months ago when Debra discovered that Joshua has began cheating on her after reading his personal emails one evening.

The couple started having regular arguments and just a week prior to her disappearance, Debra threatened to get a divorce and take sole ownership of the family house and sole custody of Alice. Joshua who is an accountant argued but was not violent toward his wife. But Debra's threat of a divorce perturbed him.

Like any other morning, Debra dropped Alice off at her school the Monday and headed off to meet one or more clients she had appointment with. As the Monday evening got older, Alice's School teacher phoned Joshua to say that Debra has not showed up for the little girl. By 6pm, with Debra's cell phone not answered by her, she was declared missing by the Lashville Police Department.

Joshua appeared genuinely worried for his wife while he conversed with police officers, Debra's father, and others in Lashville. But few of his neighbours were sceptical regarding the worried-looking husband. They have learnt about his infidelity and overheard many loud arguments he had with Debra regarding it. Some even began presuming behind his back that he might have something to do with Debra's disappearance. In the evening of the next day the thought that Debra might have been killed was strengthened when the green blouse she left home in was found on the bank of the only lake in town.

Police investigators launched a search of the lake for a body. Debra's disappearance made headline in two local newspapers. Joshua found himself been stared at as a suspect of the mysterious disappearance of his wife. Police officers questioned him on the state of his marriage with his wife.

On Wednesday of the same week that his wife went missing, Joshua was visited at 6am by 40 years old Candy Stewart, the woman he has began the adulterous affair with. Neighbours saw Candy's car drove into Joshua's driveway. Minutes later she was seen trampling from the house, getting into her car and driving off.

At 8:30am the same Wednesday two Lashville police officers knocked at Joshua's front door as he was about to leave the living room for work. Joshua answered the door and the two police officers, who knew Joshua from the years of kindergarten, told him that Candy gave them a formal report that he confessed to her about murdering his wife. One of the police officers took out a pair of handcuffs to take Joshua into custody. Appalled and carked by what is happening, Joshua slammed the door between him and the officers and dashed through the rear door.

By the Wednesday evening, the entire Lashville heard that Joshua is wanted by the police for murdering his wife. On the run, Joshua made telephone contact with his friend; a lawyer named Godfrey Jameson but refused to turn himself in to the police. By Thursday at midday, Joshua's face made headline in the two local newspapers: 'Husband wanted in case of wife disappearance,' one newspaper sated. The other stated: 'Husband on the run after confessed he killed wife.'

The Thursday afternoon Joshua decided to confront Candy about the statement   she made against him to the police. To see her, he would have to sneak his way to her house. That same afternoon as he furtively got closer to Candy's dwelling along a track, someone spotted him and called the police. While on their way to Candy's house, the police officers found Candy dead on the road leading to her dwelling. She was strangled. Joshua immediately became the prime suspect.

The Lashville police intensified their search to capture Joshua. Joshua intensified his effort to prove he is innocent of the two crimes now pressed against him, working mainly with Jameson, the lawyer. Alice in the meantime is taken in by Debra's father.

On Sunday morning of the next week, a man called the police and told them he saw Joshua entered Candy's house. On their arrival, the police officers caught Joshua standing over the lifeless body of Candy's 19 years old daughter in her bedroom.

Unfolding Conclusion:

Candy had hired her male neighbour, a 56 years old former wrestler called Mack, to kidnap and kill Debra. This way Candy hoped to secure Joshua for herself. Mack, a muscular figure, did kidnap Debra on the Monday morning but found himself liking her very much; he hid her away in the basement of his own house.

On the Wednesday morning when Candy visited Joshua, she thought Mack had killed Debra. Thinking that Debra is dead, she tried to convince Joshua to let her moved in with him and together they would raise Alice as a happy family. But Joshua disagreed and told her that the adulterous affair   was a foolish act and that it should have ended long ago. Resentful and felt used,   Candy decided to destroy Joshua by lying to the police that Joshua confessed to her he had killed his wife and dumped her body in the lake.

When Debra's body was not discovered in the lake, Candy confronted Mack about where he had put the body. Mack revealed that he had not killed the married woman and was keeping her for himself. Inflamed by what she was told, Candy clouted Mack across the back of his head with a metal candlestick to kill him. Still conscious and strong after the blow, Mack retaliated by strangling her with his bare hands. He then dumped her body on the side of the road leading to her house, just few minutes before Joshua was seen heading to Candy's house along a track at the back. The approach of the police repulsed him.

Mack was having sexual relationship with Candy's 19 years old daughter. Early the Sunday morning Debra managed to free herself from Mack's basement. She knocked at the nearest house for help, which turned out to be Candy's house. Candy's daughter let Debra in and Debra phoned Joshua right away. While dialing the phone number of the Lashville Police Department, Debra explained what happened to her to the 19 years old girl. Candy's daughter then learned that Mack was holding Debra captive.

As someone from the Lashville Police Department answered the phone, Mack suddenly appeared behind Debra and pulled away the telephone, ending the call. He pulled Debra into another room and locked her in alone. Candy's daughter, who is crazily in love with Mack, confronted him   about having another woman locked in his basement.   Knowing the girl could not keep his secret, Mack strangled her with his bare hands.

When Joshua turned up at Candy's house around five minutes later, in response to Debra's call, he found Candy's daughter dead on the living room floor. The police then caught him standing over the dead body.

A car trace with Mack's van and the Lashville Police ended at the border of the town. Debra who was trapped in Mack's van was not hurt. Mack was taken into custody and confessed to the murders of Candy and her daughter and the kidnapping of Debra.

Joshua is now a free man and is still married to Debra and raising their daughter, Alice.

Six

The Mexican Drug lord

52 years old Marco is wanted by the Mexican police for masterminding illegal drug trafficking and wanted for questioning in the cases of more than ten murders across Mexico. In April as police special operations put inevitable pressure on his drugs trading business and turfs, Marco is forced to take flight from his hiding place in the east of Mexico City to the West. He conceived a plan to have himself transported in a casket decorated with wreaths in the back of a hearse.

On April 28, three of Marco's top men accompany him to a funeral home where the clandestine journey begins. Two hearses leave the funeral home after 2pm, one believed to be holding Marco. At 4pm the hearse has not turned up at the destination. By 7pm it is clear that the drug lord is missing. What had happened to him?

The Plot:

Marco is head of the most organized and equipped, illegal drugs trade in Mexico. His organization is built up of not only civilians but police officers, nurses, judges, and politicians. He even had the president of the country on his side. But when a new Mexican president came to power with new policies, Marco began to see parts of his illegal drugs and guns trade crumble under his feet.   A new police task force to fight illegal drugs and guns trafficking was put in place with new types of raids. Corrupt politicians are getting arrested, captured illegal drug dealers are interrogated through torturous methods; some killed, and rewards are offered by the new government to informers.

Marco is facing new challenges than before. One of his top men was recently killed not very far from his place of abode, and this incidence hinted to the new and aggressive government that he might be in the east of the capital city. Marco figured his personal security is threatened. He felt galvanized by the recent events to move his secret residence to the west of Mexico City. With his face already known by everyone who watches the news, Marco announced to all his top men, numbering nine, that he will be transported in a hearse to his new secret residence.

On April 28 only three of Marco's top men accompanied him to a funeral home where the plan was for him to get into a casket and commence the private journey. At almost 3pm, the hearse bearing the white casket along with another hearse dive out of the funeral home. The three accompanying top men drove behind the hearse in a red Mitsubishi motorcar.

About five minutes in the journey, the Mitsubishi got stopped by two police officers.   While the police checked the documents of the driver, all the three men have to watch the hearse carrying their boss disappear in traffic. After handing back the documents, the police officers allowed the Mitsubishi to resume the journey. The driver desperately tried to catch up with the hearse   but reached the planned destination without a sight of the funerary vehicle.

By 7pm the drug lord is considered missing. All the top men in his organization are perturbed. They rushed few investigations with no satisfactory result. There is no news that the police have captured Marco. The owner of the funeral home says that the hearse has not returned. The top men wondered if a Cartel gang had moved against their boss.

At 8:05 pm 42 years old Franco, Marco's right hand man, announces that the hearse was found at the cemetery that the other hearse from the same funeral home went. Marco, the casket, and the driver are missing from it. The hearse bears no sign of an attack. It has no blood, no gunshot holes, and no evidence of forced entry.

Around 5 am the house Marco has departed is raided by members of the new military-styled police task force. The officers found an empty house. The raid further proved to the top men in Marco's organization that he is not in police hands. This left them to suspect the Cartels. Several phone communications led by 35 years old David, one of Marco's top men, gained no information that the drug lord was taken by a Cartel gang.

David meets with Franco in a restaurant to discuss his different speculations on the worrying situation of their missing boss. Franco tells David that two of his speculations make sense and instruct him to invite the other seven top men to Marco's new residence for a serious discussion on the road ahead if it turned out that the organization lost Marco.

David agrees and all the other top men of the illegal drugs and guns organization are invited to Marco's new house on the west border of Mexico City close to 12 midnight. At 12: 30 am police officers raided the house and all eight men, including David, are killed in a shootout. Five police officers also lie dead by a grenade thrown by one of the top men.

Conclusion:

Marco came to the decision that the only way to save his illegal drugs and guns trading organization was to run it by himself. Before the deaths of the eight top men in the west of Mexico City, Marco had to make important decisions and share net profits with them. Now he is the sole boss. To get to this position, Marco concocted a clever plan:

Before he got into the casket at the funeral home, Marco shared a 'thank you drink' with the hearse driver. The drink was laced with a poison to kill the driver within two hours.

The two police officers who stopped the three men driving behind the hearse were paid by Franco to do so in order to allow Marco out of the men's sight. Along the way the hearse driver got dazed by the poison in his body. When he stopped the hearse, Franco, who was following the hearse in a blue car, took him out and put him in the blue car and left him in it to die there. Franco then drove the hearse to the cemetery where he and Marco disappeared with the casket.

That same evening Marco had Franco give instruction for all the eight other top men to gather at his supposed new dwelling where the police officers were set up on them to exterminate them. Having all those top men killed, Marco now runs the illegal drugs and guns trade with more money coming to him and his right hand man, Franco.

Within one week Marco had the new president of Mexico assassinated and restored normal business activities within the organization he had started 15 years ago.

Seven

The vanished Corpse

At 11:54 pm a group of middle-aged, late night diners on the third balcony of an apartment complex heard a scream from the second balcony. One female diner took a look from the third balcony and saw a motionless figure resembling a young woman in the garden. She alerted the other diners who began looking down in the garden many feet below. Suddenly the lights in the garden went out, the garden engulfed with darkness, and when the garden lit up again 30 seconds later, the motionless figure on the ground had disappeared.

Few minutes after 6 am the next morning, the owner of the apartment complex called the police. His 19 years old daughter, Claudia, had gone missing from her room on the second floor.

Was the motionless figure seen in the garden the body of the 19 years old girl? And if so, how did it disappear during the several seconds of darkness in the garden?

The Plot:

56 years old George Abraham is the owner of the large apartment complex. His wife Julia is currently abroad on a business trip, leaving him and their 19 years old daughter called Claudia. Both father and daughter had regular,   heated arguments over

Claudia's way of dressing and her romantic relationship with a 27 years old shiftless guy called Mike.

Mr. Abraham wanted Claudia to stop seeing Mike, because he is an ex-convict and recidivists who uses crack and cocaine and committed break-ins. But Claudia was deeply in love with her boyfriend and was stubborn against her father's advice, even after few incidences of visible physical abuse while been out with Mike.

Mr. Abrahams had no legal means to stop his 19 years old daughter from seeing her boyfriend. He tried to have Mike prosecuted for the physical assaults; he tried to take out a restraining order against him, but without the support of his daughter, he failed miserably.

Mr. Abraham banned Mike from his apartment complex and warned him to stay away from his daughter. But a daredevil with control on Claudia's emotion, Mike sneaked unto the property and got to Claudia's room more than once in the night.

On the Friday night that Claudia went missing, one elderly tenant says he saw the young woman going toward the garden at around 11: 30pm. Two tenants claimed they sighted Mike leaving the compound of the apartment complex at 11:45 pm. After climbing over the fence, he got on his motorbike and rode off.
The same two tenants, a couple, claimed that at 12 midnight they saw Mr. Abraham drove from the grounds of the apartment complex in his car.

The small group of tenants who were dining on the third floor of the building claimed they saw what appeared to be the body of a young woman at 11:54 pm and it disappeared from the garden within 30 seconds later when the light briefly went off and back on.

By 9am the Saturday morning Claudia's body was found in a dumpster near the house Mike lives. She was hit on the head with a blunt object.

Conclusion:

Based on eyewitnesses' accounts, Mike met with Claudia at 11:30 pm in the garden and left at 11:45pm. The diners on the third floor heard Claudia screamed and glimpsed her body lying in the garden at 11:54pm. This means that Claudia was alive after Mike was seen leaving the compound and rode off alone on his motorbike. This means that Mike is not the killer.

But what about the fact that Claudia's body was found near Mike's dwelling?

Mike did not return to the apartment complex that Friday night, and Claudia was never seen leaving the compound after Mike rode off. This leads us to our other suspect—Mr. Abrahams.

Mr. Abrahams was seen by the two tenants driving out in his car at midnight. This is six minutes after Claudia's body was glimpsed in the garden. Mr. Abrahams is the killer, and we figure out how events unfolded that Friday night as follows:

Mr. Abrahams found out that Mike was with Claudia in the garden. Going to the garden, he picked up the blunt object to confront Mike. But when he got to the garden, Mike had already left several minutes before. He confronted Claudia and a physical struggle ensued during which she screamed out before been struck in the head by the blunt object.

Claudia fell dead in the garden. Mr. Abrahams rushed toward a switch that controls the light in the garden. It was at this point that one of the diners on the third floor, followed by the other diners, looked down and saw the body. Then the light went out, Mr. Abrahams hurriedly removed the body and switched back on the light.

Thinking of a way to get away with the murder of his own daughter, he tried a clever move. He put the body in his car and was seen driving out at midnight. He dumped the body in a dumpster near Mike's dwelling to frame him. But he failed to frame Mike.

Eight

Dead Witness

24 years old Lizzie Lurksome was the sole prosecutor's witness in a jewelry looting case to be tried two days before she went missing from her room at her mother's house. The police found the sheet on her bed and the floor stained with her blood, the panes of the window to her bedroom broken, and shoes prints of a second person on the grounds outside her bedroom window.

Two days later on the date of the trial, the prosecutor was to declare no case against the defendant, 32 years old Tedroy Blake, as the crown witness is missing and considered dead. Tedroy was to walk free from the courtroom.

Did Tedroy have Lizzie, whose testimony would have put him in prison for a long time, murdered? And if murdered, where is the body?

The Plot:

Tedroy and Lizzie have been lovers since she was age 23. They met while Lizzie was an employee at Chung's Jewelry Shop. That day Tedroy came into the jewelry store with a gold watch to sell. Lizzie was the first to greet him. When their eyes met it was love at first sight for Lizzie. She slipped him her cell phone number on a piece of   paper along with his receipt. Five days later the handsome Tedroy rang her phone and their romantic relationship commenced.

As the romantic relationship strengthened and both began trusting each other more and more, Lizzie learnt that her boyfriend is a computer hacker. He told her and at first she felt rather mesmerized by the information. He told her he is a computer hacker who gets hired by companies to test the security of their computer systems. Realized that Lizzie is blinded by romantic love and open minded, Tedroy figured she would make an excellent partner of crimes.

A computer hacker who was never actually hired by any company to test their computer system, Tedroy steals credit card information stored online, captures card numbers through fake online stores, and scammed PayPal. He then used the funds to purchase expensive jewelry and sell them to legitimate stores and on the black market.

Tedroy coaxed Lizzie into an act she would have thought of as unthinkable by her. But romantic love inundated her, plus Tedroy is the adventurous type that many young women tend to admire. Tedroy got her to agree to help him rob Chung's Jewelry Shop. The plan was easy: Tedroy instructed her to press the Chinese man's shop keys on two bars of soap. He later had copies of the keys made. At 1am Sunday morning of the next week Tedroy entered the shop and stole all the jewelry, valuing almost four million dollars.

Within two weeks later Tedroy sold off the jewelry on the black market. Lizzie was given $200,000 for herself. Then she made the mistake which got her boyfriend arrested. She posted a picture of a gold ring from Tedroy in a group chat on a mobile phone application called WhatsApp. Because she was still an employee of Chung's Jewelry Shop which got robbed, some individuals suspected that the ring was from the loot. Someone informed the police.

Police officers searched the house Lizzie lived but found nothing incriminating. When the police officers left the house, Lizzie telephoned Tedroy who immediately removed all incrimination items from his apartment. As Lizzie hung up the phone her mother was standing behind her through most part of the telephone call.

Less than one hour later police officers were back at the house. Lizzie's mother pressured her in front the officers to speak the trust. Under pressure, Lizzie told the officers that her boyfriend looted the store. She refused to say more. The officers searched Tedroy's apartment and found two gold watches. Tedroy was arrested on suspicion of breaking in and stealing.

Tedroy's lawyer, a friend and also a dealer on the black market, secretly met with Lizzie within two hours after Tedroy's arrest. He told Lizzie that because the watches bore no mark of ownership by Chung's Jewelry Shop, the prosecutor is depending on her testimony to link the watches to the Chinese man's shop and Tedroy to the loot. He advised her not to give a sworn statement before the court hearing and to sate that she was pressured by her own mother to state to the police her mother's assumption that her boyfriend looted the store.

A day before the court hearing, Lizzie went missing.

Conclusion:

One minute into the court hearing, Lizzie turned up at the court. The prosecutor was glad to see her. But then Lizzie spoke to the prosecutor's disappointment. She told the judge that two men kidnapped her from her house because they thought she knew that they were the actual thieves of the jewelry from the shop. She told the judge that she begged for her life, while been blindfolded, and told the men that she was going to court to testify against a man named Tedroy Blake. Not knowing the named man, the men let her go.

She then told the judge what Tedroy's lawyer had instructed her to say. Considering the matter, the judge dismissed the case.

Nine

Death of a Soldier

43 years old former United States soldier, Gary Allen, is found dead in the living room of his home in Los Angeles, California with a single gunshot wound to the right side of his head.

Gary was on medication for depression. His wife Lindsay for the first time publicly said he spoke about committing suicide. But did he commit suicide? Gary was left-handed. It is not possible, or it is most unlikely, for someone to use his left hand and shoot himself through the right side of the head.

His wife was the only one with him at the house at the time the gunshot was heard by neighbours. Did she kill him? And if yes, what would have been her motive?

The Plot:

Gary was an affable, outgoing and sociable man who was also adventurous. He joined the United States military 15 years ago, married his long time sweetheart 12 years ago, and less than one year ago was honourably discharged from the army after losing a leg and an eye in an explosion overseas.

Though given the respect and appreciation by the army for his long years of service, after five months back home David became depressed. He was not the man he physically and facially used to be. Few children called him names of a cartoon character when they see him on the streets, and the pictures with his former handsome face negatively affected his emotions.

A friend from childhood days named Austin Smith convinced Gary to start attending the church he is the pastor of. Gary's wife was already a member of the church. So he felt it was easy to fit in with the members and make new friends. But instead of things getting better, it got worst.

A female member of the church told Gary that his wife has began a sexual relationship with Austin while he was overseas on military duties. She told Gary that Austin has had several sleepovers at the house. Gary at first dismissed the information as true. Austin is a very caring guy and Lindsay is a hospitable woman. Both were most likely meeting at the house for Bible studies, he concluded. Though he gave no serious thought to the information from the female church member, Gary could not erase it lingering in the back of his mind.

The possibility that his wife was cheating on him while he was away serving the best interest of his country could not be considered entirely false. Gary knew about surprises. Through the years he was a soldier, he has experienced very amiable individuals who were spies for enemies and safe-looking plots that turned out to be booby trap.

One Sunday afternoon after church service, Gary observed Lindsay shook hands with Austin. The way they looked at each other got him suspecting they might have more than just a friendship going on between them. That same Sunday afternoon at home Gary, who got around easy with a crutch and had sprained his left wrist in the morning during a slip and fall, starred his wife in the face with his one left eye and asked her if she has cheated on him with the pastor. An argument was then overheard between them by neighbours. Soon after the heated argument the gunshot that killed Gary was heard by the neighbours.

Conclusion:

The immediate assumption by the neighbours was that Lindsay shot Gary. It is easy to see how and why the neighbours had this immediate belief. They all heard the angry argument less than two minutes before the sound of the gunshot. But the crime scene evidence differed.

Gunpowder residue was not found on any of Lindsay's hands but was detected on Gary's right hand. The pistol was registered to Gary and was carried around by him. Already a sufferer of depression, Gary shot himself using his right hand because his left wrist was sprained.

Ten

The Bedroom Tragedy

The police were called to 16 Beckford Street few minutes past 9pm after 40 years old David Blaine's wife said she found him stabbed to death in the master bedroom at the family house. A neighbour, Miss Wilton, claimed she saw 30 years old Mark Williams sneaked into David Blaine's bedroom around 9pm and then hurried out about half of a minute later.

Mark Williams was arrested for the murder at 1am the following morning at his home one mile away. But why would Mark want David dead?

The Plot

Four weeks before his tragic death, David started a media promotion for his men's shoes business. He approached an advertising agency to do an advert. The agency put together a fascinating ad using a young male model named Mark Williams. David had seen Mark more than once before. They lived only a mile from each other. But at the time of doing the ad for his shoes business, it was their first time personally meeting. They quickly became friends.

David and Mark's friendship grew intense within days, and both men went to sports events together, talked a lot by phone, and soon Mark began making visits to David's house.

David was married to Marsha for two years and the couple were raising David's daughter whom he had with a woman from a previous marriage. Within the last seven days of David's life, the couple began having arguments after Marsha found out David had commenced sexual activities with the handsome Mark. She discovered this one day when she listened to a voice message from Mark on David's cell phone.

Still living in the matrimonial home but not speaking and not sleeping in the same bedroom, the couple at least agreed on one thing that their middle-aged neighbour, Miss Wilton, would take care of David's 5 years old daughter while he was at work. Marsha's temporary refusal to take care of the little girl, whom she described in anger as David's responsibility, seemed to the 5 years old girl like the act of a no-good stepmother. So 60 years old Miss Wilton began coming over to the house to care for the girl while David was at work.

On the night of the murder, Miss Wilton had left after David came home. Marsha had cooked dinner only for herself and gone to her room. Around 8:30pm David put the little girl to sleep in her own room. Then he went to the master bedroom. At 9pm Mark sneaked over to the house and climbed up to the window of David's bedroom. The window was deliberately left ajar by David. He was expecting Mark that Friday night, like previous Friday nights, for sexual intercourse.

By 9:15pm David's house on Beckford Street was a crime scene for police investigation. Miss Wilton's witness statement put Mark at the house that night.
When police officers woke Mark out of bed early the Saturday morning, he admitted that he did sneak into the house but vehemently claimed he never committed the murder. If he did not kill David Blaine, the police officers reasoned, why did he rush home without telling anyone? This logical reasoning along with the witness statement put Mark in custody for the crime.

As detective Williams, an uncle of Mark, investigated the crime, he saw David's wife as the second person likely to have committed the murder. Days leading up to the murder, she was in enmity with her husband. The white night dress she was wearing when the police arrived had blood stain at the tail. The knife used to kill the victim had her finger prints. The knife was from the kitchen in the house, and so Detective Williams figured it would thus have the wife's finger prints. She was cooking in the kitchen in the evening.

The more Detective Williams investigated was the more his nephew looked less guilty of the murder. Mark's own words and Miss Wilton's witness statement put Mark at the crime scene, but the crime scene does not put Mark in the position of the murderer.

Detective Williams figured that the witness statement from Miss Wilton served to clear Mark of the murder instead of painting him as the killer. According to Miss Wilton, she saw Mark entered David's bedroom through the window   and rushed out in less than a minute. The detective figured that it was impossible for Mark to have entered David's bedroom, walked through it, go downstairs to the kitchen, find a knife, and then returned to the bedroom, stabbed David five times, and then leave the house under a minute. But Marsha could, the detective theorized, because she was already in the house.

Base on the fact that Marsha's finger prints were on the murder weapon, trace of the victim's blood found on her night dress, and that she was the only one known to have ample time to get the kitchen knife, Detective Williams had her arrested for murder. Mark was then freed of the charge.

But just one hour after the arrest of Marsha, Detective Williams came upon a piece of evidence that shocked everyone.

Conclusion:

David Blaine was recording his love-making sessions with Mark Williams every Friday night. On the night of his murder, he had already set up the hidden camera in the master bedroom and set it to record. The recording shows David sitting at the computer in his bedroom when the killer crept up behind him with the kitchen knife at 8:53pm. The killer, wearing a pair of gloves, plunged the knife into David's nape followed by three stabs to the side of the neck and one to the upper back. David slumped lifelessly at the computer desk. The killer then turned and walked out of the bedroom. The hidden camera clearly captured the killer's face. It was Miss Wilton.

When arrested and showed the video footage of her killing David Blaine, which she could not argue, Miss Wilton confessed to the murder.   Her motive?

She stated that she killed David because he was a homosexual whose abomination was destroying his marriage and corrupting the mind of his daughter. This explanation would not save her from prison.

Miss Wilton realized that Mark was making clandestine visits to David's bedroom after seeing him entered through David's bedroom window on two previous Friday nights. She became aware of David's homosexual affair after a conversation with Marsha. To save a wife and a little girl from David's so-called corrupting influence, Miss Wilton decided to kill David and as a result get rid of Mark.

Because the middle-aged neighbour was given the job to care for David's daughter, she had access to the house. She secretly made a copy of the front door key. On the Friday night, she gained entrance to the house before the time Mark normally arrived, went to the kitchen and pussyfooted to David Blaine's room and killed him.

Nigel D. Salmon is a Jamaican author and literature
speaker. Website: **www.NigeldSalmon.com**

www.ingramcontent.com/pod-product-compliance
Lightning Source LLC
Chambersburg PA
CBHW030542290526
45786CB00004B/1826